WATCH ME WALK

Let GOD order your steps,
and start walking in your purpose.

BY

JENNIFER HILL

ISBN: 978-0-999-5562-0-7

Copyright 2018 by Jennifer Hill

All rights reserved. Except for use in any review, the reproduction or utilization of this work in whole or in part in any form by any electronic, mechanical or other means, now known or hereafter invented, including xerography, photocopying and recording, or in any information storage or retrieval system, is forbidden without the written permission of the publisher, Summerland Publishing, 887 Hanson Street, Bozeman, MT 59718. For more information, visit www.SummerlandPublishing.com.

Printed in the U. S. A.
Library of Congress Number: 2018931383

Layout and Design by Pizzirani Consulting

A MESSAGE FROM THE AUTHOR

Matthew 24:35 KJV

Heaven and earth shall pass away,
but my words shall not pass away.

Scriptures referenced in this book are from several versions of the Holy Bible:

King James Version

New International version

Message Bible

English standard version

I salute you all with a Holy kiss.
> *Love the Lord with all thy heart.*
> *Learn from my mistakes.*
> *Take heed to my advice.*

*Never let your temporary heartache turn
into chronic pain.
Weeping may endure for a night, but joy comes
in the morning!
Expect great things; for as a man thinketh in his heart,
so is he.
Actions speak volumes; therefore, act out of love.
When you fall, get back up!
Say your blessings.*

DEDICATION

I dedicate this book to my son Tyler, and my daughter Destiny. Thank you for all of our late-night conversations about the power of prayer.

I thank GOD for you both each and every day!

#prayerchangesthings

CONTENTS

Introduction 7
Chapter I: Dear Sisters 9
Chapter II: What's Your Name? 13
Chapter III: Put Your Shades On 18
Chapter IV: Jaywalking 23
Chapter V: Walking on Quicksand 26
Chapter VI: Running Back 32
Chapter VII: Stumbling in Stilettos 37
Chapter VIII: Falling Down 41
Chapter IX: On the Bench 46
Chapter X: Street Walker 50
Chapter XI: Walking in the Rain 53
Chapter XII: Via Dolorosa 56
Chapter XIII: Bow Down 61
Chapter XIV: Walk the Runway 65
Chapter XV: Push Your Way Through 68
Chapter XVI: Daughter of a King 72
Chapter XVII: Walk and Talk with Jesus 76
Chapter XVIII: Walk in Excellence 79
Chapter XIX: Walk Your Walk 82
Chapter XX: Last Page 86
About the Author 88

INTRODUCTION

PURPOSE

The reason for which something was created.

"Before I formed thee in thy belly, I knew thee; and before thou cameth forth out of the womb, I sanctified thee and I ordained thee a prophet unto the nations." Jeremiah 1:5

God has a wonderful purpose for each and every one of us.

Jeremiah 29:11 reads,

"For I know the thoughts that I think toward you, saith the Lord; thoughts of peace, and not of evil, to give you an expected end."

You—yes you—were created for a very specific purpose. When you start feeling discouraged, lost or unsure, remember you were created on purpose.

Ephesians 2; 10 tells us we are his workmanship created in Christ Jesus unto good works which God hath before ordained that we should walk in them.

Unfortunately, many of us spend our time running with this world instead of walking in our purpose.

#WATCHMEWALK

CHAPTER I:

DEAR SISTERS

The bible tells us that a woman's worth is far above rubies and diamonds. Unfortunately, many of us are running in this world, presenting ourselves like a cubic zirconia instead of a diamond. Do you know why you cannot present yourself as a cubic zirconia? The answer is simple; a cubic zirconia is weak and fake. A cubic zirconia is artificial. When something is artificial, it is produced by man, rather than occurring naturally. A diamond, on the other hand, is strong—so strong that it can cut!

We all want to be diamonds, but don't forget a diamond begins as coal and carbon. It must endure a process of extreme heat and pressure. Instead of enduring the pressure, we end up giving up on the process and settle for being a cubic zirconia. We settle for less than Christ-like behavior from ourselves and from others. We say things like, "It's okay, God knows my heart." God does know your heart, but God's word tells us to seek him with all our heart.

Instead of seeking God with all our heart, we give our heart to the world. We make excuses for our behavior, and try and justify it by making statements like, "I have been through a lot." Sisters, maybe those difficult things you went through were meant to turn your weakness into strength; your carbon into diamond.

Instead of enduring the process of heat and pressure, we end up succumbing to everything vain. We do what the world tells us to do, instead of what the word tells us to do. We go shopping on a Saturday morning for a Saturday night outfit to go clubbing in. We purchase the shortest outfit the world tells us to wear, and then we sleep in until noon on Sunday because we are hungover.

Instead, we should go shopping for a Sunday outfit and go and dance for the Lord; He is the reason we are able to dance in the first place. We wake up in the heartbreak hotel next to a man whom we don't even know his last name.

Sexual sin is very serious. **Corinthians 6:18** tells us to flee from sexual immorality. All other sins a person commits are outside the body, but whoever sins sexually, sins against their own body.

Proverbs 31 says that when a man is married to a virtuous woman, he will be known in the gates when he sitteth among the elders of the land; It does not say a woman will be known because of who she is married to.

We crave to be treated like our worth is far above rubies and diamonds, and it is; but how can we expect to be held in such a regard when we present ourselves as weak, fake and artificial?

Dear sisters…

We must change our walk

#WATCHMEWALK

CHAPTER II: WHAT'S YOUR NAME?

When my girlfriends and I would go out to the nightclubs, we would use fake names. My fake name was Candy. Men would approach me and ask me what my name was, and I would put a sinful smile on my face, purposely flashing my pearly white teeth and reply, "My name is Candy."

While many of us run around in the world using fake names, God will show up and change your name even if He has to wrestle with you. Have you ever been wrestling with who you are? Beloved, do not forget God knows us by name.

Isaiah 43:7 reads,

Even everyone that is called by my name; for I have created him for my glory, I have formed him; yea, I have made him.

Take the story of Jacob in the bible. This is the saga in which we find Jacob. Jacob was on a journey to his father's land in Canaan in an attempt to make amends with his brother Esau. Esau possessed the honor of being older brother of Jacob, which gave him the right to a double portion of their father

Isaac's inheritance, but Jacob tricked his father into giving him the inheritance that was due to Esau. Upon Jacob's travels to Canaan, he wrestles with God and receives the new name of Israel.

Genesis 32:24-29 reads,

And Jacob was left alone, and a man wrestled with him until the breaking of the day. When the man saw that he did not prevail against Jacob, he touched his hip socket and Jacob's hip was put out of joint as he wrestled with him. Then he said, "Let me go, for the day has broken." But Jacob said, "I will not let you go unless you bless me." And he said to him, "What is your name?" and he said, "Jacob". Then he said, "Your name shall no longer be called Jacob, but Israel, for you have striven with God and with men, and have prevailed!" Then Jacob asked him, "Please, tell me your name." But he said, "Why is it that you ask my name?" And there He blessed him.

Jacob had been wrestling with God mentally for a very long time, and when God showed up and wrestled with him physically and touched his hip and it was put out of joint, it was there that He blessed him and his life was changed forever.

I too was mentally wrestling with God at this time in my life. I was very vain. To be vain is to be conceited and proud of pretty things. I was elated with a high opinion of myself, especially my almost perfect straight white teeth. Just like when God showed up and touched Jacob's hip and his life was changed forever, God showed up and touched my face and my life was changed forever too.

The dance club was closing, and my girlfriend handed me the car keys and stated she was leaving with a man. I should have called another ride or took a taxi as I was severely intoxicated, but I decided to drive. I was speeding at the rate of 95 miles per hour on the highway, and I was about to miss my exit, so I turned the steering wheel to the right as fast as I could in an attempt to make the exit, causing a horrific accident. My legs were stuck under the steering wheel, and my face hit the dashboard so hard I began spitting out teeth. But our God is so merciful, He had strategically placed an ambulance just three cars behind me, and by His grace I learned a life lesson, and He let me survive.

I lost twenty pounds because I couldn't eat solid food. I had stitches in my face, and had seventeen dental visits to correct my once almost perfect straight white teeth.

I never called myself "Candy" ever again. What's your name?

Let God change your name and start walking in your purpose…

#WATCHMEWALK

CHAPTER III: PUT YOUR SHADES ON

God wants us to have a happy life filled with joy and prosperity.

Jeremiah 29:11 reads,

"For I know the thoughts that I think toward you saith the Lord, thoughts of peace, and not of evil, to give you an expected end."

There are things in this world to give us pleasure while here on earth. For many of us, pleasures of the world become our focus. We cannot be devoted to both God and this world. Loving the world means being devoted to the world's temporary pleasures and philosophies. Sometimes we get consumed by what the world has to offer, and we cannot see clearly.

Sunglasses are a great fashion accessory, but their most important job is to protect your eyes. Some of the sun's effects on the eyes include cataracts, a clouding of the eye's lens that blurs your vision. You must put your shades on while navigating your way through the world.

John 2:15-17 reads,

"Don't love the world or things of the world. If anyone loves the world, the love of the father is not in him. For all that is in the world—the desires of the flesh and the desires of the eyes and pride in possessions—is not from the father but is from the world, and the world is passing away doing its desires, but whoever does the will of God abides forever."

The world will try and convince you into believing in relativism. Relativism is the belief that there is no absolute truth.

Beloved readers, I assure you;

THERE IS ONE ABSOULTE TRUTH AND HIS NAME IS JESUS.

John 14:6 reads,

"Jesus is the way, the truth and the life."

The world will try and influence you into believing in rationalism, also known as "the scientific method." This is a theory that if something cannot be proven through a repeated experiment, it's not considered to be true.

Hebrews 11:1 reads,

"Now faith is confidence in what we hope for and assurance about what we do not see."

If you don't have your shades on, the world will attempt to convince you into being a conformist. A conformist is someone who conforms to accepted behavior or established practices.

Romans 12:2 reads,

"Do not be conformed to this world, but be transformed by the renewal of your mind, that by testing you may discern what is the will of God, what is good and acceptable and perfect."

The world will try and lure you into calling yourself a postmodern person. Post modernity is a world view and it teaches people to refuse to allow any single defining source for truth. It is a pessimistic mood of skepticism and uncertainty.

1Kings 8:60 says that all the people of the earth may know the Lord is God, and that there is none else.

1Corinthians 3:19 reads,

"The wisdom of this world is foolishness in Gods sight."

Don't let your vision become clouded and blurred. Don't lose sight of the steps God has ordained for you. Put your shades on and start walking in your purpose.

#WATCHMEWALK

CHAPTER IV:

JAYWALKING

I got a ticket the other day for jaywalking. Jaywalking is when you cross or walk in the street unlawfully or without regard for approaching traffic. Many of us are jaywalking in life. We do whatever we want, sometimes unlawfully and without regard for approaching traffic.

Do you know what can happen if you have no regard for approaching traffic in life? You can end up in a head-on collision. We say things like, "I live in the moment." We make snap decisions out of fear. We take shortcuts. We hustle. We make permanent decisions based on temporary situations. We choose to walk on the wicked paths of the world.

Proverbs 4:26 reads,

"Give careful thought to the paths for your feet and be steadfast in all your ways."

The worldly paths are dark and dangerous and full of evil. Don't be tempted to jaywalk in these ill ways. The paths of the righteous are filled with love and light.

Stop jaywalking and start walking in your purpose.

#WATCHMEWALK

CHAPTER V: WALKING ON QUICKSAND

Watch Me Walk Jennifer Hill

I was in Florida one summer when I was unexpectedly introduced to quicksand. I was walking along a swampy area behind my grandmother's house playing around having fun in what I thought was sand. I felt my feet begin to sink and I panicked and began thrashing around, which only made the situation worse.

There was a time in my life when I was partying on the weekend a lot. I justified my behavior by saying I was just having fun. The partying quickly turned into a lifestyle and I began to sink.

When confronted, I panicked and began to thrash around. After I got tired of being sick and tired, both physically and mentally, I found an antidote to this poisonous behavior. My antidote was memorizing scriptures. I felt closer to God when I was able to achieve my goal of memorizing a scripture. One of the scriptures that really resonated with me was:

1 Corinthians 10:13

"No test or temptation that comes your way is beyond the course of what others have had to face. All you need to remember is that God will never let you down; He will never let you be pushed past your limit; He will always be there to help you through it."

I once read a book called "The Illustrated Art of Manliness." It had a six-step guide to escaping quicksand. I started applying these six things to my life, and everything changed. I believe we should all apply these six step principles to our daily lives.

1) Know your enemy; you won't sink unless you panic.

Peter 5:8 tells us to be watchful of the enemy.

"Be sober minded; be watchful, your adversary, the devil prowls around like a roaring lion seeking someone to devour."

2) *Don't panic when you are faced with the enemy, instead remember:*

2 Timothy 1:7

"For God hath not given us the spirit of fear; but of power and love, and of a sound mind."

3) *Move slowly*

The beginning of **Jeremiah 2:25 reads**

"Slow down; take a deep breath, what's the hurry? Why wear yourself out?"

4) *Loose the extras. If you are carrying dead weight it may hinder your chances of getting out.*

Give your burdens to God.

Hebrews 11:28-30 reads,

"Come to me all who labor and are heavy laden, and I will give you rest. Take my yoke upon you and learn from me, for I am gentle and lowly in heart and you will

find rest for your souls. For my yoke is easy and my burden is light."

5) *Get your legs free.*

Free yourself from sin.

Ephesians 4:31 says,

"Get rid of all bitterness, rage and anger, brawling and slander, along with every form of malice."

6) *Lean backwards*

Lean on God.

Proverbs 3:5 reads,

"Trust in the Lord with all thine heart; and lean not unto thine own understanding."

STOP LEANING ON THE WORLD AND START LEANING ON THE WORD.

7) *Get out*

Get out of harm's way.

2 Corinthians reads,

"Therefore, come out from among unbelievers and separate yourselves from them says the Lord."

Get out of the quicksand and start walking in your purpose.

#WATCHMEWALK

CHAPTER VI: RUNNING BACK

Watch Me Walk *Jennifer Hill*

At one time in my life, I was in a relationship that I thought would last forever. I dreamed about my fluffy white wedding dress and believed we would live happier ever after. I thought we had a lot in common. I was a poet and he was a musician. We both admittedly had abandonment issues, and had both been severely hurt from previous relationships.

I thought we had the ultimate love story. We spent every waking moment together and sleeping moments too. We waited for each other every night and never went to sleep unless we were lying next to each other. From the day we met each other, we never spent a night apart.

Just because you have a lot in common does not mean you are supposed to be together. Sometimes, you are attracted to one another because of your bondage. Bondage can be a controlling force of lust of your own flesh.

John 6:63 says,

"The spirit gives life; the flesh counts for nothing. The words I have spoken to you they are full of the spirit and life."

To further explain, spiritual bondage can be any area of our lives in which we come into agreement with the world by disregarding God's word.

When we were together, our behavior was disastrous. We would stay up indulging in marijuana and liquor for days at a time. I would call in to work and fabricate stories as to why I could not come in that day. My boyfriend wouldn't show up to meetings that had been set up for months in advance, which was detrimental to his career. We found ourselves in a pattern of behavior in which we were constantly seeking approval from one another.

Our self-worth became dependent on one another. We were becoming co-dependent. I believed we had a lot in common, but what we really had in common was our pain.

We would break up for a spell and run right back to each other. We would move on opposite sides of town and tell each other it was over, but within weeks one of us would break our lease and go move in with the other one. You can't expect God to bless your household while you are shacking up.

GOD IS NOT THE AUTHOR OF CONFUSION.

After years of running back to one another, I finally ended it by asking myself one question.

IS HE GOOD FOR MY PURPOSE?

Even though I was not sure of what my purpose was at that moment, I knew the answer was no, and I wasn't good for his purpose either. When God created Eve, He created her to be a helpmate for Adam. If I was good for my boyfriend's purpose, I would have been encouraging him to attend his meetings.

WE WERE IN A WORLDLY RELATIONSHIP WITH EACH OTHER INSTEAD OF A RIGHTEOUS RELATIONSHIP WITH GOD.

Stop running back and start walking in your purpose.

#WATCHMEWALK

CHAPTER VII: STUMBLING IN STILETTOS

I stumbled and sprained my ankle while wearing my favorite pair of stilettos. I didn't stumble because of the height of the shoe; I stumbled because I was inebriated.

There is a line in one of my favorite movies.

"SERIOUSLEY, IF YOUR'E ALWAYS IN A CHEMICALLY INDUCED STATE, YOU MIGHT WANT TO RECONSIDER EVERYTIHING THAT YOU'RE DOING; AND THINKING TOO."

It should have come as no surprise that I stumbled. At the time my thoughts were distorted, and the behavior that I was exhibiting was pure dissipation.

Have you ever noticed a lot of liquor stores are named "Wine and Spirits?" Maybe you have noticed a complete change in someone's (or your own) personality after they have consumed too much alcohol.

Studies show after a certain level of consumption of liquor, you are no longer in control. Some people have reported other spirits entering their body. When the alcohol wears off and one's level of consciousness raises again, people reported the spirit departing from their body.

When people report being drunk and blacking out and not remembering dancing on the table, it's because it was not their spirit who was dancing.

We are warned of these dangers in **proverbs 23:30-35:**

"Those who tarry long over wine; do not look at wine when it is red, when it sparkles in the cup and goes down smoothly. In the end it bites like a serpent and stings like an adder. Your eyes will see strange things, and your heart utter perverse things.

You will be like one who lies down in the midst of the sea, like one who lies on the top of a mast.

'They struck me' you will say but I was not hurt; they beat me, but I did not feel it. When shall I awake? I must have another drink."

This passage speaks to the temporary moments while intoxicated where you don't feel anything. I assure you, when the alcohol wears off, you end up feeling horrible.

Beware of strong drink and any other mind-altering intoxicants. Be sober so that you may hear clearly from God.

Stop stumbling in your stilettos and start walking in your purpose.

#WATCHMEWALK

CHAPTER VIII: FALLING DOWN

Proverbs 24:16 tells us:

..a righteous man falls seven times and riseth up again, but the wicked shall fall into mischief.

The word righteous denotes one who is holy in heart. In Hebrew, the word for holy is "quadosh". The word means to be separated from all that is unclean. Holiness, therefore. is a separation from the corruption of the world and set apart for God.

The word *wicked* in this content is a mental disregard for virtue. Some describe wicked as evil in thought. Seven is a number that signifies completeness. The righteous man falls seven times and gets up again; by contrast the wicked are assured that they have the upper hand but they end up getting trapped by their own wickedness when they fall.

King David's life exemplifies what we read in **Proverbs 24:16.**

King David was the greatest of Israel's kings. He ruled over the largest territorial reign in their history. In **Samuel 1:1,** we see that it was in the spring of the year; the time when kings went out to battle, that David was still in the palace; not in battle position.

David was not where he was supposed to be. Have you ever been in a place in life where you were not supposed to be? All that would follow may have never happened if David had been where he was supposed to be.

While David was in the palace, he committed adultery and impregnated another man's wife. This woman's name was Bathsheba. Bathsheba was married to a man named Uriah. Uriah was a loyal solider in King David's army.

David ate and drank with Uriah after this adulterous act took place, and made Uriah drunk on purpose in hopes that he would go home and sleep with his wife so that Uriah would believe that the child Bathsheba was pregnant with was his.

Uriah was so loyal, he did not go home. He slept at the door of the palace with all the servants instead.

David then conspired to have Uriah killed by having him carry a sealed letter to Jacob that contained orders to have Uriah placed in the forefront of battle, and then have the forces draw back to ensure Uriah would be killed.

This seems incomprehensible for the king of Israel, but that is how sin works. One sin leads to another sin in attempt to cover up the first sin. David's sinful plan worked. David was responsible for Uriah's death. David had surely fallen, but our God is so merciful.

WHEN WE FALL, GOD DOESN'T GIVE UP ON US.

We give up on ourselves, but God's love never fails. When we repent and cry out to God, He hears us. Are you where you are supposed to be? David was forgiven by God, and if we sincerely repent, we too can be forgiven when we fall down.

In **Psalm's 51:1,** David cries out to God, "Have mercy on me, O God, according to your steadfast love; according to your abundant mercy; blot out my transgressions."

When you fall, repent, get back up and start walking in your purpose.
#WATCHMEWALK

CHAPTER IX: ON THE BENCH

I started playing baseball when I was eleven, and I was an awful player. I sat on the bench most of the season. My baseball stance was unbalanced and when I was up to bat, it really bothered me when the catcher would taunt me with her evil words. She would say things like, "You're not good enough" or "You should quit."

My teammates didn't make it any better. They would never cheer for one another and were negative all the time. When I was allowed to play, I was lost in left field. At the end of the season, I told my mom I was quitting baseball, and that I never wanted to play again. I said, "I have no purpose on a baseball team."

DO YOU EVER FEEL LIKE QUITTING? ARE YOU STRUGGLING WITH DISCOVERING YOUR PURPOSE?

My mom was adamant about not letting me give up. She said, "You just need a different atmosphere." She switched me to another team for the following season and demanded that I practice every day.

I was hesitant at first. I didn't have any brothers or sisters to practice with, so I began to practice by myself. I watched everything I could on television about baseball. I studied the art of a good batting stance, and I practiced throwing the ball against the side of the house every time I was outside.

When the new season began, I felt great! My teammates were positive and cheered one another on. During the first game, I stood up at the mount and my stance was close to perfection. I was so mentally focused on hitting the ball, that I couldn't even hear the catcher's voice.

I hit my first homerun that day! I was so good at throwing and catching because I had practiced on the side of the house so much. This season, instead of being lost in left field, I was on third base.

Think about this. It is the same process when it comes to discovering your purpose. Sometimes, you have to change teams. You have to surround yourself in the right atmosphere. You must position yourself around positive people.

ARE THE PEOPLE YOU ARE SURROUNDING YOURSELF WITH CHEERING YOU ON?

Are you surrounding yourself with positive or negative people? You have to study God's word, even if you have to study by yourself.

You have to make sure your stance in life is balanced so that the world can't taunt you. You must be mentally focused so that when the world tells you that you are not good enough, you ears and conscience won't even hear those words.

Get off the bench and start walking in your purpose.

#WATCHMEWALK

CHAPTER X: STREET WALKER

The world will tell you prostitution is the oldest profession in history, as if that somehow makes it okay. Many people will try and justify being involved in this circle by saying things like "the money is good". Beloved readers don't forget that all money is not good money.

Timothy 6:10 reads,

"For the love of money is a root of all kinds of evil. Some people, eager for money, have wandered from the faith and pierced themselves with many griefs."

Sisters, when God created you surely He did not say to himself, "her purpose while on earth will be streetwalking." Brothers, when God created you, surely He didn't say to himself, "his purpose while on earth will be pimping women." Streetwalking destroys the spirit and soul in a way that can lead to physical and spiritual death. Please, turn away from these sinful acts.

Romans 6:23 reminds us that the wages of sin is death, but the free gift of God is eternal life in Jesus Christ our Lord! All of us have the opportunity to receive salvation and eternal life from God and to be cleansed from our unrighteousness.

Proverbs 10:2 says,

"Tainted wealth has no lasting value, but right living can save your life!"

Stop streetwalking and start waking in your purpose.

#WATCHMEWALK

CHAPTER XI: WALKING IN THE RAIN

Taking a walk in the rain often makes a person feel negative and gloomy, but taking rainy day walks regularly helps train your mind to think positive and go about this beautiful thing called life, no matter what storms we may face.

Remember, rain helps things grow. I was walking in the rain one day, and I was feeling negative and gloomy. I plopped down right in the middle of the road and let the tear drops run down my face like the falling rain. It was at that very moment that I heard God ask me a question. He said, "Daughter, where is your faith?" He spoke to me again, and asked, "Have I ever left your side?" His words put a childlike smile on my face and I hopped up and started jumping in the rain puddles.

This encounter made me think about the time when Jesus and his disciples were literally in a huge rainstorm. (**Mark chapter 4 verse 38 and verse 40**) Jesus had gone to sleep on the boat while the disciples stayed awake. Instantaneously they found themselves in the midst of a huge storm. The rain was frantically pouring down and the waves were violently splashing up against the boat and eventually the boat began filling up with water.

The disciples panicked and ran to wake Jesus up they said, "Teacher, don't you care if we drown?" Jesus awoke and rebuked the wind and said to the sea, "Peace be still." Suddenly, the wind stopped and there was a great calm.

Then, Jesus asked his disciples, "Why are you so afraid? Have you still no faith?"

When storms arise in our lives, the world teaches us to be afraid and feel gloomy. The enemy wants us to plop down and give up.

Beloved readers, Jesus will never let you down. The next time you are faced with a huge storm, jump in the puddles with a smile on your face and then start walking in your purpose.

#WATCHMEWALK

CHAPTER XII: VIA DOLOROSA

Watch Me Walk *Jennifer Hill*

The Via Dolorosa is a street within the old city of Jerusalem believed to be the path that Jesus walked on the way to his crucifixion. Some refer to this path as the path of pain. I believe many of us are walking in pain and instead of making a left, we stay on the painful path and punish ourselves.

When the black plague spread across Europe in the thirteenth and fourteenth centuries, people publicly whipped themselves with irons in bloody processions of self-flagellation.

When we are wounded, we often see ourselves as the sum of our inadequacies. We privately punish ourselves behind closed doors and speak ill over our own lives. We publicly punish ourselves by walking around angry, so the entire world can see the disappointment in ourselves. Beloved readers, that is not God's will for our lives.

When Jesus walked down the Via Dolorosa, he was severely beaten along the way.

Isaiah 53 reminds us that:

BY HIS STRIPES WE ARE HEALED.

"But he was wounded for our transgressions; he was bruised for our iniquities. The chastisement for our peace was upon Him and by his stripes we are healed."

Once upon a time in my life I took the things that had wounded me and began to punish myself. I told myself that it was my fault my biological parents gave me away, because

I wasn't worth keeping. I told myself that it was my fault that I was date-raped. I should have never agreed to go out with him. I told myself it was all my fault that boy called me chubby; I should have had more self-control. I felt unworthy.

In addition to punishing myself, I became obsessed with being the best at everything. I literally made myself sick. I had to be the best employee. I had to be the skinniest woman in the room. I had to be worth it. Before I even realized it, I had developed an eating disorder and was a workaholic starving for perfection.

I tortured myself. After two years of this frenzied behavior I was checking the mail when a bright neon sticky note fell out of the mailbox. I bent down to grab it, and I felt so dizzy that I just sat on the ground for a moment. I held the note in my hand and when my equilibrium felt normal again I read it. It said:

"He heals the broken hearted and binds up their wounds."

I felt like God was talking to me through that neon note.

GOD TURNED MY WOUNDS INTO SCARS AND I STARTED TO LOVE MYSELF FROM THE INSIDE OUT.

I BEGAN TO HEAL.

I started to write down the things that I did like about myself on bright sticky notes, just like the one I found falling out of the mailbox, and I placed them all around my apartment. I began to speak life over myself.

One night, I wrote down all of the things that had wounded me on small scraps of paper. I wanted to use scraps of paper because the things that I allowed to hurt me for so long, I now considered scraps.

MY WOUNDS HAD NO POWER OVER MY LIFE ANYMORE!

I sat in front of the fireplace and burned each scrap of paper one by one.

Stop punishing yourself. Stop walking on the path of pain and start walking in your purpose. Jesus already walked the Via Delarosa for you.

#WATCHMEWALK

CHAPTER XIII: BOW DOWN

2 Kings 17:35 says;

"With whom the Lord made a covenant and commanded them saying, 'You shall not fear other gods, nor bow down yourselves to them nor serve them nor sacrifice to them.'"

Beloved readers, we must ask ourselves how much clearer can these instructions be. Many of us find ourselves bowing down and worshiping the things of this world as if they were God. We bow down to our jobs, our possessions and even to other people.

We listen to music that demands us to "bow down" to the performer. Take heed to this warning. This is very dangerous. The bible advises us over sixty times about the dangers of having false gods and idols.

In Abrahamic doctrines, a false god is a deity or object of worship that is regarded as either illegitimate or non-functioning in its professed authority or capacity; and this characterization is further used as a definition of an idol.

Remember the story in the Bible about the huge gold statue. King Nebuchadnezzar demanded that everyone bow down and worship it. The three men who refused to do so, Shedrach, Meshack and Abednego, were thrown into a fiery furnace and King Nebuchadnezzar commanded that the furnace be heated up to seven times its normal heat.

God is so amazing! He covered these three men. The men were not hurt at all by the fire. When you trust God, you will discover that He will never leave you nor forsake you.

Daniel 3:23 reads,

"But look; he said I see four men walking around freely in the fire completely unharmed! And the fourth man looks like a son of the gods."

It's no wonder that the worship of false gods is called harlotry in the bible, since the relationship between man and the false gods is so closely akin to prostitution. A price is paid, and a service is rendered, but there is certainly no love between the two parties.

False worship is one of the greatest evils man can practice. The greatest commandment of all Jesus said is:

"LOVE THE LORD YOUR GOD WITH ALL YOUR HEART AND WITH ALL YOUR SOUL AND ALL YOUR MIND."

Stop bowing down to the things of this world and start walking in your purpose.

#WATCHMEWALK

CHAPTER XIV: WALK THE RUNWAY

The first thing you are taught when walking the runway is that if you fall down, you must get back up. It doesn't matter if you are embarrassed, uncomfortable or even hurt, the show must go on.

Another thing that is required is to hold your head up high; hence practicing walking around the room with a book on top of your head. This method is a part of an etiquette lesson in poise and gracefulness.

You have to apply these things in your daily life as well. When you fall down, you must get back up no matter what you are feeling. Life is full of embarrassing, uncomfortable and hurtful moments, but it is in these moments that you draw closer to God.

Romans 5:3-4 says

"Not only so, but we also glory in our sufferings, because we know that suffering produces perseverance; perseverance, character; and character, hope."

The show must go on. It is inevitable that you most certainly will fall down in life and when you do you must get back up and hold your head up high, both physically and mentally.

HOLD YOUR HEAD UP HIGH, FOR YOU ARE A CHILD OF GOD!

Walk the runway of life with poise and gracefulness and start walking in your purpose.

#WATCHMEWALK

CHAPTER XV: PUSH YOUR WAY THROUGH

The textbook definition of the word *push* is a vigorous effort to do something, demand persistently, or to exert one to attain something.

When you start walking in your purpose, you cannot be apprehensive. You must push through all of the trials and tribulations that you are faced with.

Hebrews 11:1 reminds us of how very important our faith must be.

"Now faith is the assurance of things hoped for, the conviction of things not seen."

YOU ARE GOING TO HAVE TO STOP LEANING ON THE WORLD AND START LEANING ON THE WORD.

You must push through the noise and barricades the world will put up against you. Remember, this world is temporary. This world will pass away.

Take the story in the bible regarding the woman who had the issue of blood. She physically pushed her way through the crowd until she was close to Jesus. She pushed herself mentally and tapped into her faith saying to herself, "If I only touch his garment I will be made well."

Consider the stage in which this woman was in. She had a bleeding condition and the issue had continued for twelve years. She was considered invalid to those around her. She had spent all of her money on treatments from several doctors and nothing had helped her condition.

Jewish law declared her to be ceremonially unclean due to her bleeding issue. According to this law, anything she touched became unclean as well.

Matthew 9:20-22 reads,

"And behold a woman who had suffered from a discharge of blood for twelve years came up behind him and touched the fringe of his garment for she said to herself, 'If I only touch his garment, I will be made well.' Jesus turned and seeing her said 'take heart daughter; your faith has made you well.' And instantly the woman was made well."

The last words Jesus speaks to her are so tender. He calls her daughter. He teaches her that the power of her faith healed her. Your faith must be unshakable.

Faith requires confidence.

Push through the calamity of the world and tap into your faith.

Push your way through the crowd and start walking in your purpose.

#WATCHMEWALK

CHAPTER XVI: DAUGHTER OF A KING

2 Corinthians 6:18 reads,

"And I will be your father and you will be my sons and daughters saith the Lord almighty."

While you may have encountered less than father-like behavior from your dad, rest assured because you are the daughter of a King.

Don't make a series of self-defeating mistakes because you may have an emotional void from your earthly father.

Our heavenly Father will show you the most loving kindness a father can have for his daughter.

YOU ARE DIVINLY SAFE AND PROTECTED.

No rank is so elevated as that of being the daughter of the Lord almighty! I believe many of us forget who we are in Christ.

Psalms 91:1-13 reminds us of the covering over our lives by our Lord.

"You who sit down in the high God's presence, spend the night in shaddais shadow say this; God you are my refuge! I trust in you and I am safe!"

He rescues you from hidden traps, shields you from deadly hazards. His huge outstretched arms protect you—under them you are perfectly safe—his arms fend off all harm.

Fear nothing: not wild wolves in the night, not flying arrows in the day, not disease that plows through the darkness, not disaster that erupts out of high noon. Even though others succumb all around, drop like flies right and left, no harm will even graze you.

You will stand untouched—watch it all from a distance; watch the wicked turn into corpses.

Yes, because God is your refuge, the high God your very own home, evil can't get close to you; harm can't get through the door.

HE ORDERED HIS ANGELS TO GUARD YOU WHEREVER YOU GO.

If you stumble, they'll catch you; their job is to keep you from falling. You'll walk unharmed among lions and snakes and kick young lions and serpents from the path.

*YOU ARE THE DAUGHTER OF A KING!
STOP FORGETTING WHO YOU ARE AND
START WALKING IN YOUR PURPOSE.
#WATCHMEWALK*

CHAPTER XVII: WALK AND TALK WITH JESUS

Matthew 11:29 reads,

"Walk with me and work with me—watch how I do it. Learn the unforced rhythms of grace. I won't say anything heavy or ill-fitting on you."

Our savior is simply saying believe in him, hearken to him as a teacher and rely on him as your personal Lord and savior.

1John 15:7 says,

"If you abide in me, and my words abide in you. You will ask what you desire, and it shall be done for you."

We make it difficult for ourselves to walk and talk with Jesus but it's not difficult at all. He wants us to have that intimate bond with him. He wants our walk to be so much like his that we will be in unison with him.

In the world of music, unison is two or more musical parts sounding the same pitch or at an octave interval, usually at the same time. When this happens, beautiful harmony occurs.

Not only does Jesus want us to have a life filled with beautiful harmony; he wants is to create it.

Walk and talk with Jesus and start walking in your purpose.

#WATCHMEWALK

CHAPTER XVIII: WALK IN EXCELLENCE

When you are walking in excellence, you won't be received by everyone. Some people will be so happy to see you shine and for others, your shine will be so bright it will hurt their eyes.

People that at one time adored you might not like you anymore. When people operate out of hate, you must do the opposite and operate out of love like Jesus did.

Colossians 1:11 reminds us to utilize the strength that has been given to us.

"Being strengthened with all power according to his glorious might so that you may have great endurance and patience."

When you are walking in excellence, the devil will try and set up road blocks and obstacles all around you in an attempt to trip you up, both physically and metaphorically.

No matter what hurdle you are faced with, you must jump over it.

Remember what **Peter 2:9** tells us,

"But you are a chosen people, a royal priesthood, a holy nation, God's special possession, that you may declare the praises of Him who called you out of darkness into His wonderful light."

Walk in excellence and start walking in your purpose.

#WATCHMEWALK

CHAPTER XIX: WALK YOUR WALK

Walk your walk. Jesus says no one comes to the Father except through me.

IT'S NOT ABOUT RELIGION; IT'S ABOUT YOUR OWN PERSONAL RELATIONSHIP WITH JESUS.

Colossians 2:13-23 in the message bible reads,

"When you were stuck in your old sin-dead life, you were incapable of responding to God."

God brought you alive, right along with Christ. Think of it. All sins forgiven! The slate wiped clean, the old arrest warrant cancelled and nailed to Christ's cross. He stripped all the spiritual tyrants in the universe of their sham authority at the cross and marched them naked through the streets.

So, don't put up with anyone pressuring you in details of diet, worship services or holy days. All those things are mere shadows cast before what was to come;

THE SUBSTANCE IS CHRIST.

Don't tolerate people who try to run your life, ordering you to bow and scrape, insisting that you join their obsession with angels and that you seek out visions. They are a lot of hot air, that's all they are.

They're completely out of touch with the source of life, Christ, who puts us together in one piece whose very breath and blood flow through us. He is the head and we are the body, we can grow up healthy in God only as He nourishes us.

So then if with Christ you've put all pretentious and infantile religion behind you, why do you let yourselves be bullied by it? Don't go near this. Do you think things that are here today and gone tomorrow are worth that kind of attention?

Such things sound impressive if said in a deep enough voice. They even give the illusion of being pious and humble and ascetic. But they're just another way of showing off making yourself look important.

Walk your walk, not anyone else's. Start walking in **YOUR** purpose.

#WATCHMEWALK

CHAPTER XX:

LAST PAGE

When you start walking in your purpose everything changes…

Your wardrobe changes
The way you speak changes
Your behavior changes
YOUR WALK CHANGES

So, if you see changes in me, know it's because I am walking in my purpose.
#WATCHMEWALK

ABOUT THE AUTHOR

Jennifer Hill is an outgoing evangelist, who has been described as the ultimate humanitarian. She brings encouraging words to the world.

Jennifer was adopted as an infant and has a special place in her heart for children. You can find some of her work featured in the *Highlights* magazine for children.

Jennifer is a professional motivational speaker and specializes in youth and women's events. You can book Jennifer for an upcoming event via her website:

www.jhill-straightupevangelist.com

Summerland Publishing also offers these two additional devotionals by Jennifer Hill on Amazon.com and BarnesAndNoble.com as well as your favorite bookstore:

Girlfriend Let Me Remind You   ***Sanguine***

www.ingramcontent.com/pod-product-compliance
Lightning Source LLC
Chambersburg PA
CBHW071733040426
42446CB00012B/2341